N-F

Finding Out About
LIFE IN BRITAIN
IN WORLD WAR I

Cherry Gilchrist

Batsford Academic and Educational   *London*

Contents

© Cherry Gilchrist 1985
First published 1985

All rights reserved. No part of this publication may be reproduced, in any form or by any means, without permission from the Publisher

Typeset by Tek-Art Ltd, Kent
and printed in Great Britain by
R J Acford Ltd
Chichester, Sussex
for the publishers
Batsford Academic and Educational,
an imprint of B. T. Batsford Ltd,
4 Fitzhardinge Street
London W1H 0AH

ISBN 0 7134 4817 2

ACKNOWLEDGMENTS

The Author and Publishers would like to thank the following for their kind permission to reproduce illustrations and copyright material: BBC Hulton Picture Library for the illustrations on pages 7, 23 and 43; Robert Beard for the illustrations on pages 30 and 37; Buxton Museum for the illustration on page 29 (right); Imperial War Museum for the illustrations on pages 8, 9, 11, 17, 20, 21, 25, 26, 29 (left), 33, 36 and 39 (right); P.H.B. Lyon for "Now to be Still and Rest" on page 43 from *Turn Fortune*, published by Constable; Quaker Archives for the illustration on page 19; B.J. Saunders for extracts from the letters of Robert Saunders on pages 6, 8, 32-3, 35, 38 and 42. The map on page 44 was drawn by R.F. Brien. The illustrations on pages 13, 15, 31, 34 and 39 (left) are from the Author's collection.

Frontispiece

The changing role of women: road sweepers in Ealing during the war years (Imperial War Museum).

The colour illustration is of a munitions factory (Imperial War Museum); the two black and white illustrations are (left) children outside a coal depot (BBC Hulton Picture Library) and (right) an advertisement for Bird's Custard from the Sphere *1 September 1917 (Robert Beard).*

Introduction

From August 1914 till November 1918, Britain was at war with Germany. This was known at the time as the "Great War", though it is now usually referred to as the "First World War". Germany was at that time a very powerful nation, allied to Austria-Hungary, and was seen by Britain as a threat to the peace and stability in Europe. Britain was also in a strong position, ruling a large Empire which included countries like India and Australia. Her chief allies in the war were France and Russia, later joined by Italy and the United States. The reasons why war actually broke out are very complicated, but there are two key events which triggered it. The first happened on 28 June 1914, when an Austrian Archduke, heir to the throne, was assassinated by terrorists. Austria reacted aggressively and her ally Germany was soon involved. In August 1914 German troops invaded Belgium, and this serious disruption of peace provoked Britain into declaring war.

The patriotic spirit in Britain was extremely intense during the war, and most people believed that Britain was right to fight. The outbreak of war was welcomed as a chance to show Germany what British troops were made of, and to bring a greater glory to the British Empire. There was a belief that the war would be over by Christmas at the latest, and Lord Kitchener, Minister for War, shocked the Government when he said that it would take about three years to fight and would require a million men. In fact, even he did not foresee that the war would last four years and that five million men would be needed in the armed forces.

During the war, about a quarter of all the men and boys in Britain went to war. This meant great changes in the way of life of those left at home. Many women had to cope with looking after families on their own, and often, as well, to suffer the grief of losing a husband, brother or son in the war. As the war went on, there were great labour shortages, but this gave women new opportunities to take jobs in industry, agriculture and the professions.

For both the women at work and the men in the army it was a chance to meet people of different social classes. Before the war, society in Britain was divided very rigidly into different classes, and although the war did not break down the class barriers completely, it changed the patterns and brought people closer together. Upper-class women gained a greater freedom to work, to wear simple dress (even trousers!) and to run their own lives. Lower-class women no longer had to take badly paid jobs as servants or dressmakers since there was plenty of well-paid work on offer. They were able to feed their families better, and, in general, the health of poorer families improved tremendously during World War I. (Many lower-class men were rejected as unfit for the army because their health had been spoilt by a poor diet, appalling living conditions and over-strenuous work.) Women showed their resourcefulness and talents so well during the war that in 1918 Parliament was finally persuaded to give women (but only those over the age of 30) the vote, something for which the "suffragettes" had been campaigning for many years.

Communications during the war became very important, and newspapers, photographs, the cinema and even telegrams displayed in Post Office windows were used to get out the news of the latest events in Europe as fast as possible.

The Government took control of certain features of life in Britain during the war, including a large section of industry: it ran munitions factories where shells, bullets and so on were made, it cut down the number of hours that pubs could stay open, regulated food supplies, took over control of transport and increased income tax to pay for the war. Paper money was printed for the first time, to get over the problems caused when people started to hoard their gold and gold coins.

There had been industrial unrest and strikes just before the war, and to make the running of industry easier during the war the Government asked workers not to strike, and even made strikes illegal in key industries. In 1915, however, the South Wales miners defied this rule and the Government were forced to come to an agreement with them rather than to use the law to punish them. During the war, trade union memberships increased so that by 1918 about a third of all workers were union members, instead of about a quarter in 1914.

In general, the population was eager to help the war effort, and many people spared their time and money to help make equipment or take on extra duties. Special Constables (a volunteer force) patrolled the streets and helped to guard key points, such as power stations which might be attacked by the enemy. Scrap metal and other "salvage" that could be used in making weapons or vital supplies was collected carefully. People gave up their cars and sometimes even their homes to be used for war work, such as nursing the wounded.

The war dragged on far longer than anyone expected; in 1914 it had seemed a glorious cause, but by 1918 it appeared a futile and tragic one to many people. They hoped that it would be the last great war that Britain would ever have to fight, but, of course, in 1939, the Second World War was to destroy this belief. The first Armistice ("Remembrance") Day took place in 1920, and we still hold it each November in memory of the men who died in both world wars.

Try to find a history atlas, such as *The Times Atlas of World History*, which will show you how big the British Empire was at the time, the boundaries of the European countries, and where the important battles of World War I were fought.

═Useful Sources═

1. PEOPLE AND ORGANIZATIONS
a) *Librarians* Ask the librarian at your local or district library if there are any photos or documents or newspaper cuttings to do with World War I. There may be a special collection relating to your area. Your librarian may also be able to tell you if there are any plans for an exhibition of local history — very often people in the neighbourhood bring in their own souvenirs and photos for displays like this, and some of them will probably relate to the First World War.

b) *Teachers* Teachers at your school can tell you whether there are any school records or photos from the period that you can look at. Perhaps there are old school magazines dating from 1914-18; you will find examples of these in this book.

c) *Local organizations* Try contacting your local British Legion organization (your library will give you the address) to see if they have any material that might be of interest. British Legion work is mainly to do with providing help for people who were left disabled or suffering after both World Wars. It would also be worth writing to your local Women's Institute or Townswomen's Guild, as some of their members may have taken an interest in collecting memories and records of life during the First World War.

d) *Relatives and neighbours* Anyone with clear memories of the First World War must be at least seventy-five today, so perhaps there is someone among your older relatives or neighbours who can remember what life was like then. You may be able to make a tape recording of their recollections. If your school or youth club gives any community help to elderly people, you could take the opportunity to ask if any of them has stories to tell about the war.

2. VISUAL MATERIALS
a) *Photographs* Look for photos of the World War I period in your local reference library, museum and even family albums. It can be hard to find interesting pictures of the time, since people tended to pose in a formal way for photos.

b) *Museum displays* The Imperial War Museum in London, and some local museums, have displays covering life in World War I. Many museums contain far more material than they are able to put out at once, and the curators are often happy to help people who want to work on a special project.

c) *Postcards, cigarette cards and advertisements* At collectors' fairs or in junk and antique shops you can often find examples of World War I postcards and cigarette cards. They may be humorous or serious, are often colourful, and can show all sorts of interesting details about life at the time. Advertisements may appear on postcards, or as separate sheets, or be included in magazines or newspapers of the period.

d) *Memorials and inscriptions* War memorials, many in the form of crosses, are often found near churches or at a central point in a district, such as the town square or village green. Some buildings, such as town halls and railway stations, may also have inscriptions dedicated to the men who died in the First World War. (Many now stand in memory of both World Wars.) Can you find out about the most famous war memorial in London, and the occasion each year when it is honoured?

3. WRITTEN SOURCES

a) *Newspapers and magazines* Your local library will probably have some newspapers or magazines of the 1914-18 period. These can make fascinating reading; try to find examples of both local and national papers. If you read the classified advertisements you will find plenty of clues to what was going on — people being forced to sell their luxury possessions or their businesses, for instance. If there is a shop in your area specializing in military antiques, they may have some of the "war souvenir" papers which recorded the progress of the war month by month.

b) *Documents* Old ration cards, military papers belonging to soldiers, Government hand-outs and pamphlets are interesting to look at. You could find these in family collections, libraries, museums, or antique shops. Check the date if you can to make sure that they are definitely of the World War I period, since those from World War II turn up more frequently. School log books and council minutes (ask at your school or library) will give you information about what was going on in your area at the time. Records of Parliamentary proceedings (known as *Hansard*) will usually be available at your reference library and although these can be heavy-going to read, they are worth dipping into, especially to look at the question and answer sessions, which are livelier than the long speeches.

c) *Music* Perhaps some older relatives or a local antique shop have examples of sheet music from World War I. Look for patriotic songs and ones to do with soldiers, or sweethearts parting when the young man goes off to war. Most songs have the date of publication written on them. If not you will find that looking at examples in the book (see pages 9, 32 and 41) plus getting to know the fashions and styles of the time will help you to date music from the pictures on the front and the kind of printing used.

d) *Autobiography* Ask your teacher or librarian to help you find accounts which people have written about their own lives including the First World War period. Try to find out which famous writers were alive during World War I and look at the stories of their lives which either they have written themselves, or which other authors have written about them.

e) *Poetry and literature* First World War poetry has become very famous. Although much of the poetry is to do with the lives of soldiers fighting abroad, there are also poems relating to life at home in Britain. Some novels and stories written at the time or soon after also describe the changes that war brought to people's lives. Again, ask your teacher or librarian to help you find some suitable literature to look at. *Voices from the Great War* (Peter Vansittart, Penguin, 1981) would be enjoyed better by older readers, but it contains many extracts from writings of the time and a long list of authors and books which would help you choose what to look up.

The War Comes

PREPARING FOR WAR

As tension grew between Britain and Germany, people knew that war would soon break out. From his village in Sussex, Robert Saunders wrote on 2 August 1914 to his son in Canada:

We have all been in a great state of excitement. . . . All the railways are guarded, wire entanglements, trench guns, etc., have been hurriedly put round Portsmouth, and even our post office has orders to keep open day and night. Everything points to the Great War, so long expected, being on us . . .
(Saunders Letters, Department of Documents, Imperial War Museum)

Try to find out what Portsmouth is famous for, and look at its position on the map. Then you will realize why it needed special protection.

Vera Brittain recalls the scenes in Buxton, just before the declaration of war, in her book *Testament of Youth* (1933). She was twenty at the time.

Events moved, even in Buxton, very quickly. The German cousins of some local acquaintances left the town in a panic. My parents rushed over in the car to familiar shops in Macclesfield and Leek, where they laid in stores of cheese, bacon and butter under the generally shared impression that by next week we might all be besieged by the Germans. Wild rumours circulated from mouth to mouth; they were more plentiful than the newspapers, over which a free fight broke out on the station platform every time a batch came from London or Manchester. . . . One or two Buxton girls were hurriedly married to officers summoned to unknown destinations. Pandemonium swept over the town. Holiday trippers wrestled with one another for the Daily Mail; habitually quiet and respectable citizens struggled like wolves for the provisions in the food-shops, and vented upon the distracted assistants their dismay at learning that all the prices had suddenly gone up.

What do you think of people's behaviour as war approached? Do you think any of the things they did were sensible?

THE DECLARATION

Owing to the summary rejection by the German Government of the request made by His Majesty's Government that the neutrality of Belgium will be respected, His Majesty's Ambassador at Berlin has received his passport, and His Majesty's Government has declared to the German Government that a state of war exists between Great Britain and Germany as from 11pm on August 4th.

Note that the British Ambassador to Germany was brought home as a sign that friendship between the two countries had been broken off.

"PRACTICAL PATRIOTISM"

On 6 August 1914, *The Times* published suggestions for "Practical Patriotism", which included:

Keep your heads. Be calm. Go about your ordinary business quietly and

Crowds gathered outside the Houses of Parliament to hear the declaration of war. The entrance to the Houses of Parliament that you can see and the buildings look very similar today, but what about transport and the clothes people are wearing?

soberly. Do not indulge in excitement or foolish demonstrations.

Do not store goods and create an artificial scarcity to the hurt of others. Remember that it is an act of mean and selfish cowardice.

Do what you can to cheer and encourage our soldiers. Gladly help any organisation for their comfort and welfare.

Explain to the young and ignorant what war is, and why we have been forced to wage it.

Can you work out why each of these suggestions was made?

CROWD REACTION

When the news that England had declared war on Germany became known in London, there were scenes of the wildest description in the West End. In Trafalgar Square, which was impassable owing to the dense crowds, cheers were raised for the King and for England. Outside Buckingham Palace crowds once more collected and sang the National Anthem over and over again.

A hostile crowd assembled outside the German Embassy and indulged in groaning and hissing. A force of mounted and unmounted police were quickly on the scene, but had considerable difficulty in restoring order. (*Buxton Advertiser*, 8 August 1914)

Recruitment

During World War I, nearly five million men were recruited to join the British armed forces. At the start of the war, Lord Kitchener, the Minister for War, appealed for volunteers for the "New Army", and over a million men answered the call by the end of 1915. After the first excitement, though, not enough men were coming forward, and Lord Derby, put in charge of recruiting by the Government, set up a scheme late in 1915 asking men between the ages of 18 and 41 to register their names and "attest" their willingness to serve. This did not produce enough volunteers, however, and eventually, in May 1916, a Conscription Act was passed which meant that men could be called upon by law to serve in the army. This made it the first war in British history which used a large "conscript" army.

Volunteers being questioned at a recruiting office. What sort of things do you think they might be asked?

RECRUITING MEETINGS

The Parliamentary Recruiting Committee organized public meetings to try to rouse men on the streets to volunteer. Robert Saunders, up in London for a visit from his country home in Sussex, wrote to his son in Canada on 31 May 1915 about what he had seen:

> **On St Paul's Steps I watched a recruiting meeting for some time. There was a tremendous crowd round and a soldier . . . was letting out for all he was worth. He had a number of men in uniform with him and every little while stopped and pointing his finger at some man in the crowd shouted, 'Why haven't you joined?' Of course everyone looked at the victim who felt called upon to make an excuse if he could, and one of his [the soldier's] assistants pushed through the crowd to tackle the one singled out.**

What methods of persuasion was the recruiting officer using? Can you write a speech of the kind that you think he would have made?

THE WHITE FEATHER CAMPAIGN

Certain women went round the streets looking for men who were not in army uniform, and pinned a white feather on them as a sign of cowardice. (White feathers were said to be found on cockerels not brave enough to fight.) Often they offended men who were not fit medically to serve, or soldiers in ordinary clothes. Lancelot Spicer, in his introduction to *Letters from France 1915-1918*, a collection of letters he wrote to his family while in the army,

A popular recruiting poster. What information can you find in it about joining the army?

published in 1979, recalls an encounter that he had in Jermyn Street, London. He had just put his name down to be a soldier and was waiting to be called up:

As my friend and I walked down Jermyn Street together we were suddenly accosted by a little woman with a tray holding white feathers on pins. 'What are you young men doing here?' she said, in a most offensive manner, 'you ought to be out in France fighting for your country,' and with that I felt a pin being stuck onto the lapel of my jacket. I looked down to see that she had pinned a white feather on

RECRUITING SONGS

There were several recruiting songs, designed to stir the hearts of young men and encourage them to enlist in the army. Sometimes they were performed by beautiful lady singers in music halls, who offered a kiss to every man who enrolled on the spot. Here is a verse of *Your King and Country Needs You:*

Oh we don't want to lose you,
But we think you ought to go;
For your King and your Country
Both need you so.
We shall want you and miss you,
But with all our might and main
We will thank you, cheer you, kiss you,
When you come back again.

Here is a comic version of the same song. F.T. Nettleingham, who included it in his book *Tommy's Tunes,* a selection of songs collected from his fellow soldiers, comments: "A typical parody on the recruiting songs, with which the soldiers – and slackers *and* everyone else – were soon fed up."

Now, we don't want to hurry you,
But it's time you ought to go;
For your songs and your speeches
They bore us so.
Your coaxings and your pettings
Drive us nigh insane:
Oh! we hate you, and'll boo you and
hiss you if you sing it again.

Do you know any parodies of well-known songs?

me! I flung it into the gutter, but it has ever since been a great regret that I did not keep the souvenir given me by this insolent little bitch!

Home Defence

The Government were afraid that the Germans might try to land men secretly in Britain. In January 1915, Colonel Stanley Patterson, Commander of the Hamilton district, sent out a letter to local estate owners:

Confidential

My Lord/Dear Sir

As you are probably aware, we have certain information that Enemy Aircraft are working constantly in the South of Scotland.... It is probable that one of the Planes is a Hydroplane, so that its base must lie either in some sheltered part of the coast line or in one of the numerous lochs.... *I therefore venture to ask your aid in tracing the suspected base and in tracking down any foreign or disloyal persons who may be in league with the enemy.*

My suggestion is that you instruct your Gamekeepers, Farmers, Shepherds, or other reliable employees to thoroughly search, and, so far as is possible, to watch, all lochs, caves, woods or other possible hiding places on your estate and to immediately report any suspicious circumstances that may come to their notice.

Also, to observe and locate any signalling, either by Flash Light, or by means of Interchangeable Coloured Lamps (usually worked by wires on tree tops) and, if possible, to discover the Operators. (From the Department of Documents, Imperial War Museum)

Why do you think that the army asked for the help of private people in tracking down enemy agents, and do you think this could have been dangerous in any way?

The Government encouraged the public to be on the look-out for spies. Sometimes suspicious circumstances were investigated with comical results. Here, a "mysterious light" had been seen moving on a hill near Folkestone:

There could be no doubt it was an elaborate code, giving important information.... It was determined to arrest the person or persons working the signals. Very careful preparations were made; men were selected and armed as there might be desperate resistance.... It was a lovely moonlight night.... The strange light ... was located, and silently the armed men came out from their hiding places. They drew in upon the unsuspecting signaller. A moment's pause, and then, together, they dashed to the attack.... The secret was revealed in its naked truth. An allotment holder, anxious to keep birds off his ground, had conceived the brilliant idea of hanging up a piece of old looking glass. It was tied with string to a big stick. As it swung it reflected any light there was in the sky. (From *Folkestone during the War*, edited by J.C. Carlile, who also wrote the chapter from which this extract comes)

Can you think of any other ordinary happenings that might be interpreted as enemy signals?

BLACK-OUTS

To avoid the risk of attack from German airships and planes (see pages 12-13) there were restrictions on lighting used at night. Some towns, especially those on the coast, had to "black-out" their windows so that they were not visible to the enemy at night. When Vera Brittain visited her fiancé's home in August 1915, she found that:

The house was darkened. . . . All Lowestoft suffered in the same way, but they especially because the house had so many windows, and standing by itself right at one end of the town was a landmark far out to sea. They were only allowed to have lights in two rooms . . . and even in these the electric lights had to have brown paper shades and the windows thick dark curtains to cover them entirely. (*Chronicle of Youth*)

INVASION

At one stage everyone was given papers as to what we had to do if or when the enemy landed. Everyone who kept cows, pigs, etc., had to destroy them and take what possessions they could and make for somewhere inland. (Recollections noted from Miss E. Beed, 1984)

Miss Beed was living in Blean, Kent; you can see from the map that this would be a part of the country most likely to be invaded. Why do you think the people were told to destroy their animals?

Fire and ambulance services had to be kept up to scratch to cope with bomb attacks and other emergencies. As you can see, women were recruited into the fire brigade; here they are probably having a training session.

German Attacks

Although the Germans did not invade Britain, they made attacks from both the sea and the air in which altogether over 1,000 people were killed and more than 2,000 injured. Their ships bombarded towns on the East coast, and for the first time in history Britain experienced bomb attacks from the air. These came from Zeppelin airships from early 1915 to late 1916, then from aircraft, which were more effective and easier to pilot. The South and East of Britain were affected worst.

A RAID ON LONDON

One of the worst air raids on London was on 13 June 1917, when 162 people were killed and 432 injured.

I was just reaching home after a morning's shopping in Kensington High Street when the uproar began, and, looking immediately at the sky, I saw the sinister group of giant mosquitoes sweeping in close formation over London. My mother ... was anxious to watch the show from the roof of the flats, but when I reached the doorway my father had just succeeded in hurrying her down to the basement. ... The three of us listened glumly to the shrapnel raining down like a thunder-shower upon the trees in the park.... As soon as the banging and crashing had given way to the breathless, apprehensive silence which always followed a big raid, I made a complicated journey to the City.... The streets around the Bank were terrifyingly quiet, and in some places were so thickly covered with broken glass that I seemed to be wading ankle-deep in huge unmelted

AIR RAID PRECAUTIONS

People sheltered from the raids in basements, church crypts, or, in London, in tube stations. This girls' boarding school, in Bushey, Herts, made its own arrangements for air raid emergencies. Their signal for a raid was the sounding of a hooter.

Owing to the possibility of Zeppelin

ZEPPELIN RAIDS

1st April 1916 – Damage Reported
Bury St Edmunds Considerable damage to property. One man and one boy killed. 10 houses destroyed.
Braintree One house destroyed. Two damaged. One old lady missing. Six casualties.
Stowmarket Railway line blown up and telegraph wires down.
Mattishall Seven fires sighted at 11.50pm.
Sudbury Several houses wrecked. 4 or 5 lives believed lost.
Cleethorpes Billet containing 60 soldiers hit. About 40 casualties.
(From *Secret Circulars of the Air Raids*, prepared by British military staff as official reports on raids as they occurred, Department of Documents, Imperial War Museum)

Why was the damage to a railway line and to telegraph wires important?

hailstones. (Vera Brittain, *Testament of Youth*)

From this and other extracts on the page, try to describe the sequence of events in a bombing raid, and what you would do if you were there at the time.

raids we have had many new plans with regard to alarms both by day and night.

For day alarms arrangements have been made so that every form knows exactly where to go. . . . We have had two or three false alarms of this kind, and we find that the plan has worked quite well.

Miss Boys has given us two night alarms. The first, on May 27th was at about 10.45 pm, and on the following Monday, hearing the Harrow hooter, which went on for some time, we were all called out again, and we had an exciting time waiting from about 10.45 to 12.15 in the Oak room and corridor, where we had an impromptu concert to pass the time! (From St Margaret's School Magazine, summer 1915)

AIR RAID WARNINGS

It was difficult to find a safe method of giving air raid warnings. From these quotations you will see how some alarms proved dangerous.

When the attack is believed imminent . . . stations authorised to fire sound signals will fire two rockets. (Metropolitan Police 1917)

An unfortunate incident happened at Bishopsgate Street Station, Shoreditch, where a panic occurred owing to a large number of persons mistaking the Air Raid Warning Signal for bombs. Five persons were killed and seven injured in the resulting rush. (*Secret Circulars of the Air Raids*, 29 January 1918)

The British public was horrified when, early in the war in December 1914, German ships fired on Scarborough. On p. 15 you can find out how this was used to get more recruits into the army.

HEALTH RISKS

Henry Paget, Bishop of Stepney, in his book *Records of the Raids,* described health hazards apart from direct injury that could arise from air raids. What were they?

Toddlers arrive in every variety of undress. . . . One child had been dropped into a pillow-case . . . another was hastily wrapped in a table cloth. And therein lies the real danger to the children, dangers far more serious than the German bombs, of pneumonia and bronchitis and of infectious complaints. In one crypt those in charge had to isolate as best they could a child suffering from measles, and many of the clergy are now trying to persuade those with small children to remain at home, the danger of illness having become so real.

Censorship and Propaganda

Once a country is at war, its Government will usually try to make sure that its people stay loyal and committed to the cause. "Propaganda" is the term used for information which is put out with the purpose of influencing people's feelings and ideas. In World War I, the Government had a small Propaganda Bureau right from the start, but within the first year they realized that the war would need full-scale resources in terms of soldiers, equipment, money and general patriotic spirit, and so they created a Department of Information. This had several divisions, which worked to produce leaflets, films, posters and stories for the newspapers, and kept an eye on public opinion at home and abroad. The general aim of the propaganda was to show the Germans as cruel and menacing, to play up any British victories that occurred and to encourage people at home to support the war in their daily lives. To make sure that vital information did not get passed on to the enemy, the Government censored certain communicatons. Letters from soldiers abroad were censored, weather reports were not included in newspapers, as they might aid German air raids, and newspapers were forbidden to report on certain subjects, such as the whereabouts of British troops.

"CORPSE FACTORY"

The most appalling rumour of World War I (later proved untrue) was that the Germans had a "corpse factory" where they boiled down the bodies of dead soldiers to make oil. Questions were asked in Parliament; no one can be sure from the answers whether the Government were deliberately keeping this rumour going for propaganda purposes. What do you think?

> Mr Dillon asked the Chancellor of the Exchequer whether his attention had been called to the reports widely circulated in this country that the German Government have set up factories for extracting the fat from the bodies of soldiers killed in battle . . . whether the Government have any solid grounds for believing that these statements are well-founded . . .
> Lord R Cecil: With respect to this question. . . . The Government have no information at present beyond that contained in extracts from the German Press which have been published in the Press here. In view of other actions by German military authorities, there is nothing incredible in the present charge against them. His Majesty's Government have allowed the

TELEGRAMS

Censorship was in force for telegrams, which could only be allowed if they were:

> written in English or French, and on the understanding that they are accepted at the sender's risk and subject to censorship by the British authorities; that is, that they may be stopped, delayed, or otherwise dealt with in all respects at the discretion of those authorities and without notice to the senders . . . (Official ruling quoted in *The Press in War-Time*, E.T. Cook, Macmillan, 1920)

Why was French allowed, and telegrams in other languages and in code forbidden?

WHEN THE GERMANS LAND IN ENGLAND.

What is this cartoon from The Daily Mirror *(September 1914) trying to do? Why might it be called propaganda?*

> circulation of facts as they have
> appeared through the usual channels.
> (House of Commons, 30 April 1917)

"AVENGE SCARBOROUGH"

German attacks could be used as propaganda to drum up more support for the war. Newspapers were usually very glad to help. Following the bombardment of Scarborough the *Daily Mirror* reported:

> **A striking recruiting poster was being
> placarded throughout the country
> yesterday. The poster is headed
> "Avenge Scarborough", with a sub-
> head, "Up and at 'em now!" and is in the
> following terms:—
> "The wholesale murder of innocent
> women and children demands
> vengeance. Men of England, the
> innocent victims of German brutality
> call upon you to avenge them. Show the
> German barbarians that Britain's
> shores cannot be bombarded with
> impunity".
> One effect of the raid has been to
> increase materially the numbers of men
> coming forward as recruits . . .**
> (19 December 1914)

FILMS

The Government Cinema Division prepared all kinds of films, including documentaries and cartoons, for propaganda purposes. There were about 3,000 cinemas in 1914, and all the films were silent. As the cinema had not been in existence for very long, audiences tended to believe without question anything that was shown, and not realize that the camera could be used in a very selective way. Here is part of a review of a film that was on show in 1914:

> **'England's Menace'
> In this two-part picture . . . illustration
> was given as to the easy manner in
> which England might be invaded
> through foreigners being employed in
> our homes, and hostile Governments
> supplied with information regarding
> the every movement and disposal of
> our Navy and Army by spies.** (*Buxton Advertiser*, 24 October 1914)

What kind of propaganda was this film giving out, and what was it encouraging the audience to do?

Foreigners in Britain

BELGIAN REFUGEES

Many Belgians fled to Britain after the Germans invaded their country in 1914. They were supported at first by funds from the Government and charities; later many found work in factories or started their own business. In the town of Folkestone sleeping accommodation was provided for over 22,000 Belgians. When the refugees began to arrive in August 1914, many were in the state of shock, having seen relatives killed and their homes burnt. Shortly after the war, J.C. Carlile collected local people's memories and accounts into a book called *Folkestone during the War 1914-1919*, from which this extract comes:

> There on the quay was the most pathetic sight of all – little children stood clinging to big sisters for protection, or holding mother's dress with trembling fingers. They drew back in fear at the sound of a stranger's voice. . . . As the boats arrived a company of ladies met the Refugees with food and hot drinks. . . . The great majority of Refugees, when they landed at the Harbour, were practically destitute. They were taken to St Michael's Hall, where a substantial meal was served, and where those who were insufficiently clad were provided with clothing. . . . Hotel proprietors gave generously, and shopkeepers readily joined in the effort; boarding house proprietors lent or gave clothing, and beds were made up in Church halls and public schools . . .

ATTACKS UPON GERMANS

There was a public dislike of Germans who were living in Britain, and anyone who spoke German or who had a German-sounding name came under suspicion and might even be attacked. When a British passenger ship, the *Lusitania,* was sunk in May 1915, with over a 1000 lives lost, feeling in London rose to fever pitch:

> German shops were pillaged by huge and riotous crowds which the police were unable to control and men known to be Germans who showed themselves in public places were very roughly handled. The trouble began at Smithfield, where . . . a number of German butchers drove up in order to obtain supplies of meat. The meat porters in a body mobbed them and hustled them out of the market. Another German was chased across Farringdon Street into Holborn by some 300 people. . . . The English butchers and slaughterers, now reinforced, proceeded to a German barber's shop a few doors from Aldgate Station and gave him a thrashing. The shop of an Austrian barber . . . was next attacked, the mob setting about the manager, whom they seized and flung into the road. The mob looted the shop, taking possession of razors, shaving-pots, cigarettes and cigars, and practical jokers among the crowd commenced free shaving operations. (*Daily Mirror*, 13 May 1915)

Here are two accounts of life for prisoners of war. Do you think that the newspaper is giving a different point of view from that of the diary, and if so, why?

At Frimley there is a camp of German prisoners. . . . They are guarded by four rows of wire entanglements. . . . Many among them [the soldiers] looked utterly depressed, and some were stretched out on the ground or at the doors of their tents with their heads on their arms as though very weary. Others were playing cards and shouting loudly in German, some were reading, and in the distance a game of football was in progress. . . . They all appear to be very well treated. (24 September 1914, Vera Brittain, *Chronicle of Youth*)

Goose-Step Daily in Sea Prisons
Germans' Round of Pleasure on British Detention Ships

A British Seaport Town. . . . I met three National Reservists, who are doing duty on board. "Troublesome?" they repeated when I inquired about their captives' behaviour. "They are too jolly happy and comfortable for words. They have little work to do except to make their beds and do the cooking, but they just love to clean up the ship. . . . To see them do the goose-step is one of the funniest things imaginable. . . . After all, they are only too pleased to be away from the war – "I did not want to fight; I was pushed into it," confessed one prisoner; "and now I am here, I want to stop". (*Daily Mirror*, 31 December 1914)

Many foreigners living in Britain were eventually interned by the Government, partly for their own protection. Here you can see how the Alexandra Palace was turned into a camp for internees. They were allowed into the grounds, where they did some gardening They were only allowed to bring with them the barest essentials by way of personal possessions.

Objectors to the War

Men who refused to fight because they believed it to be wrong were known as "Conscientious Objectors", or "Conchies". The Conscription Act of May 1916 allowed these objectors to be excused from "combatant" (fighting) duties if they could prove that their beliefs were genuine. Tribunals (panels of between 5 and 25 men and women) were set up locally to judge each case. If a person's appeal was dismissed he would receive a summons to join the armed forces. Those who were accepted as Conscientious Objectors by the tribunals were sometimes told to take up "non-combatant" duties, such as ambulance work. In either case, if a man refused to co-operate, he was liable to be put in prison. "COs" were helped by organizations such as the No-Conscription Fellowship and the Friends' Peace Committee which advised them of their legal rights.

TRIBUNAL RULES

Nearly everyone agreed that the rules drawn up for the tribunals were fair. Here is some general guidance, given by a Mr Long, of the Local Government Board:

> While care must be taken that the man who shirks his duty to his country does not find unworthy shelter behind this provision, every consideration should be given to the man whose objection generally rests on religious or moral convictions. Whatever may be the view of the members of the Tribunal, they must interpret the Act in an impartial and tolerant spirit.

Can you think of some personal opinions which people sitting on the tribunal might have to put aside?

A TRIBUNAL AT WORK

It is estimated that between 16 and 20,000 men came before the tribunals, and that about 10,000 were successful in proving their case. Many records show that the tribunal members, untrained in law, were ignorant and predjudiced, and often broke the rules of procedure. Julian Bell visited many tribunals as a reporter and recalled in his book, *We Did Not Fight* (1933), a collection of accounts from COs:

> A young man came in and claimed total exemption from military service because he had a conscientious objection to taking human life and would not do anything to help in the war. He was asked his trade and replied he was a piano tuner. This reply was enough for the tribunal. The application was totally dismissed on the ground that no piano tuner could be a Conscientious Objector. How could he tell what uses a piano might be put to? It might be military marches and patriotic tunes?

Do you think this was fair? The writer of this piece was sympathetic to Conscientious Objectors. How might a member of the tribunal describe the case?

"PERSUADING" MEN TO JOIN THE ARMY

Pacifists who refused to turn up for military service when ordered to were first taken forcibly to an army barracks and then imprisoned if they still would not respond. This extract shows what could happen in an extreme case:

> Some of the early batches ... were taken singly and run across the yard to special rooms – airy enough but from

THE · C.O. · IN · PRISON.

"SCRUB YER TABLE, STOOL AND FLOOR."

"TAPS not to be touched by BATHERS"

THE WEEKLY

THE CHAPLAIN'S FLYING VISIT.

ON THE STOOL: A GLIMPSE INTO THE OUTER WORLD.

"GET INSIDE AN' SHUT YER DOOR."

"I WONDER IF I'M GOING MAD?"

THE VISIT — ENTENTE CORDIALE.

~1917~

Aspects of life in prison for a Conscientious Objector. Look at the drawings carefully and see why each scene represents unpleasantness and difficulty for the prisoner.

Aspects of life in prison for a Conscientious Objector. Look at the drawings carefully and see why each scene represents unpleasantness and difficulty for the prisoner.

PRISON LIFE

Objectors who refused to accept a tribunal's verdict were imprisoned. Over 6,000 were arrested during the war. Some found prison a terrible experience. J.P.M. Miller remembers his experiences in Wormwood Scrubs:

> No one who has had solitary confinement can imagine what it is like, except perhaps those people who have a fear of being buried alive. . . . When one gets to the stage of noticing a knot of wood on the floor and seeing that knot grow bigger and bigger one naturally begins to wonder whether one can hold onto one's sanity. . . . During the whole of the period I was in prison I had nightmares every night, all connected with prisons and trying to escape. . . . (From *We did not Fight*, edited by Julian Bell)

Others, such as Fenner Brockway, found consolation in acting according to their spiritual beliefs. He wrote in a letter in February 1917:

> I am thoroughly well and happy. I do not seem to be in prison. You know how contentedly I entered; that feeling has remained all through. I am calmer in spirit than I have been for a long time. . . . My cell has seemed a quiet retreat and within it I have rediscovered the power of prayer. . . .'
> (*Conscription and Conscience*, edited by J. Graham, 1922)

which they could see nothing. They were fed on bread and water and some of them presently came round. I had them placed in special rooms, nude, but with their full army kit on the floor for them to put on as soon as they were so minded. There were no blankets or substitutes for clothing left in the rooms which were quite bare. Several of the men held out naked for several hours but they gradually accepted the inevitable. Forty of the conscientious objectors who passed through my hands are now quite willing soldiers. (Lt-Col Reginald Brooke, Commander of the Military Detention Barracks, Wandsworth. *Daily Express*, 4 July 1916)

The Changing Role of Women:

Before the First World War, it was unusual for women of the middle and upper classes to work, and they would then only be employed in "respectable" jobs such as teaching and nursing. Married women of all classes did not normally work, and working-class girls tended to go into factories, shops, dress-making or domestic service as maids. From 1915 onwards, as more and more men left home to join in the armed services, women of all classes were encouraged to take up a wide variety of posts – in banking, brewing, plumbing, veterinary practice, agriculture and engineering, for example. There were even women chimney sweepers and grave diggers.

Land Work women could take permanent jobs on farms, or seasonal ones, as this advertisement shows. In what ways is the work made to sound attractive and worthwhile?

WAGES AND HOURS

Wages varied widely, from about £1 to £4 a week, but this was a lot better than the 10s or so that a maid would have been paid. Many single girls found themselves, for the first time, with money to spare for entertainment and new clothes. Here are some examples of women's employment in the city of Glasgow during the war years:

Position	Wages (weekly)	Hours worked
Lighting Inspector	31s-33s + 12s bonus	51
Lamplighters	17s-28s + 11s bonus	51
Cleaner	36s 5d	54
Electric meter reader	30s	48
Van driver	41s 6d	53½
Tram conductors	45s 6d	53½

See if you can find out how women were employed in your area, perhaps by looking at local newspapers of the time or with help from your reference library.

MINISTRY OF LABOUR ANNOUNCEMENT
WILL YOU HELP TO PROVIDE RASPBERRY JAM FOR THE FIGHTING FORCES ?
4,000 WOMEN WANTED FOR FRUIT PICKING
from the end of July to Mid-September
in the BLAIRGOWRIE and AUCHTERARDER districts

Special arrangements for fares at reduced rates.
HOUSING ACCOMMODATION ARRANGED
GOOD WAGES can be earned
MEALS can be obtained at LOW RATES in canteens.
PARTIES OF FRIENDS can be housed, fed and employed together if early application is made.
IT IS URGENT and VITAL that the fruit which is wanted for Sailors and Soldiers should be picked before it spoils.

All information and full particulars as to fares, rates of pay, equipment, etc. can be obtained from the nearest
EMPLOYMENT EXCHANGE
WHERE ALL WHO WISH TO HELP SHOULD APPLY
AT ONCE

1 – General Employment

NEW-FOUND FREEDOM

The war has brought many social changes, none perhaps more striking than that which has drawn the married women of the better classes into the ranks of the workers. . . . It is quite unlikely that after the war is over all these women, who for the first time have achieved financial independence and have tasted the sweets of liberty, will be willing to return to the old order of things. (Marie W. Seers in *Women War Workers – Accounts contributed by Representative Workers*, edited by Gilbert Stone, 1917)

Was she right? Books dealing with the 1920s and 1930s may help you to find out.

Women unloading coke for Palmers Shipbuilding Co Ltd, Hebburn on Tyne. Notice that they are wearing trousers, another change which the war brought into women's lives. They were paid between 7s 6d and 9s per day. Palmers, like some other companies, had a women's football team at this period!

PREJUDICE AGAINST WOMEN

There was resistance to the idea of women going out to work, although this grew less when the labour shortage became severe and women proved how well they could do. In rural Sussex Robert Saunders noted in a letter to his son on 4 June 1916 what was happening on farms round about as women began to work on the land.

Mr Ferner has been very emphatic about employing 'Lady' helpers on his farm, no he wouldn't etc. Now his better half says he has engaged one. You would smile to see them [the land workers], they wear thick boots, leggings, knee breeches (corduroy), a short smock, and a soft hat. . . . The one I saw would have passed for a man anywhere.

DELIVERY SERVICE

Marguerite Cardell drove a butcher's cart part-time, and was paid 14s a week.

I begin my work at 8.30am each day. My horse and cart are ready waiting on my arrival outside the shop and my first duty is to pack my cart with the meat ordered for the day. . . . My own round has from 80 to 100 calls and occupies from three to four hours daily. (From *Women War Workers,* edited by Gilbert Stone)

The Changing Role of Women:

VOLUNTARY WORK

There were many ways in which women could help the war effort directly. Voluntary work could be done for just a few hours a week – knitting garments for soldiers for instance – or given full-time in hospitals, canteens, or charity organizations. Well-paid war work was available in the munitions factories (see pages 24-25) and there were opportunities for posts in uniformed services such as the police force, the Red Cross and the Women's Army Auxiliary Corps, which from 1917 worked with supplies and catering in army camps. In its magazine for 1915-16, St Margaret's School, Bushey, recorded how some of the old girls were helping:

> **Hilda Giles is dispensing at the VAD hospital, Cambridge, in addition to her ordinary dispenser's work in a Cambridge hospital. Louise Hulbert did Pantry work in a VAD hospital in Leamington during her summer holiday.**
> **Mary Hopkins did secretarial work for the St John's Ambulance Brigade for eight months.**
> **Lena Jesson . . . helps in the mending for the 1st London General Hospital.**
> **Nina Jenkinson . . . is now doing Canteen Work in Paddington.**
> **Hilda Perry, who is teaching at St Mary's College, Paddington, does Ammunition Work on Sundays.**
> **Emily Duggan spends one day a week… packing vegetables for the Fleet.**
> **Noel Pelly helps at a Soldiers' Club in Haslemere.**
> **Viola Dickinson is in charge of a Ward at the London Hospital.**

What kind of jobs were these women doing and in what way were some of them making a special effort by doing voluntary work?

VOLUNTARY AID DETACHMENTS

VADs were founded in 1910 by the Red Cross and the St John's Ambulance Brigade. Each detachment consisted of 23 members and a commander. They became best-known for their hospital and nursing work, much of it with the troops abroad. Women "VADs" were paid a token allowance (about £25 a year) if at all. A letter to *The Times*, 10 August 1914:

> **Mrs Selby . . . Commander of Kent V.A.D. 72 . . . will be very grateful for the LOAN of a small, reliable CAR for the work of the detachment, which is on the main Dover Road and Railway and close to Sheerness, and expects to be required to take over wounded at hospitals some distance apart. Being entirely dependent on voluntary help for equipment, rations and all materials, help in money or materials of any kind is most earnestly asked for.**

NURSING

Vera Brittain broke off her studies at Oxford to become a nurse. After training, she was posted in 1915 to the 1st London Hospital, Camberwell, as a Red Cross nurse earning £20 a year. The nurses' hostel was cold, crowded, with little hot water, and the girls had to get up at 5.45 am to reach the hospital by 7.0.

> **Theoretically we travelled down by the**

2 – War Service

workmen's trams . . . but in practice
these trams were so full that we were
obliged to walk, frequently in the
pouring rain . . . the mile and half from
the hostel to the hospital. . . . We all
acquired puffy hands, chapped faces,
chilblains and swollen ankles. . . . We
tackled our daily duties with a
devotional enthusiasm now rare. . . .
Every task, from the dressing of a
dangerous wound to the scrubbing of a
bed-mackintosh, had for us in those
early days a sacred glamour. . . . Our

*Members of the Women's Police Service. They gave
general community help, such as safeguarding
women travellers and keeping an eye on children in the
streets.*

one fear was to be found wanting in the
smallest respect; no conceivable fate
seemed more humiliating than that of
being returned as 'unsuitable' after a
month's probation. (*Testament of Youth*)

Why do you think that these young women were
prepared to put up with such difficult conditions?

Munitions

Ammunition and explosives had to be made throughout the war, and during the first year it was realized that more factories and workers would be needed. This was partly because of the vast amount of ammunition used in the fighting (over a million shells might be fired in one single battle) and partly because there were not enough regular engineering workers to cope with the production anyway, since many had joined the army. In June 1915 a Ministry of Munitions was formed to organize and expand production, and they began advertising:

WORKING AT WOOLWICH AND SOUTHAMPTON

By 1916 over 500,000 women started to work in munitions, since there were not enough men available for the jobs. As a young woman of about 20, Peggy Hamilton signed on for 'three years or the duration of the war". It was a novel experience for her, since she came from a well-to-do family, but one which she enjoyed on the whole. She was sent first to the Woolwich Arsenal, in London, a huge factory covering 600 acres of land.

> I was put first onto a facing machine, turning and facing a part of the fuse cap for one of the big shells. It was easy, dull, repetitive work, and after doing the same thing for ten and a half hours daily one's speed increased. I was then put on to a capstan lathe; this was a bit more interesting, as threads, internal and external, had to be put on. . . . It was still unskilled work. . . . We never saw the shell-cases being made or the finished shell with our little contribution firmly in place. (*Three Years or the Duration – The Memoirs of a Munition Worker 1914-18*, published 1978)

Government appeals for workers
MINISTRY OF MUNITIONS OF WAR
URGENT
To British Workmen:
YOUR SKILL IS NEEDED
Shot and shell, ships and guns, munitions of war of every kind, are required. Your brothers – your pals – your fellow-countrymen are fighting for you, for King, for Empire. They must be supplied with munitions – and YOU can help to supply them. There are thousands of skilled men who are burning to do something for King and Country. By becoming a War Munition Volunteer each of them can 'do his bit' for his homeland.
Get into the Factory Line and supply the Firing Line
WAR MUNITION VOLUNTEERS ARE URGENTLY WANTED
Men! Go at once to the
MUNITIONS WORK BUREAU
When you have enrolled you will be notified where your help is required, but you will not suffer in wages, and provision is made . . . for the payment of travelling expenses and lodging money where necessary.
ENROL TODAY.
(Extracts from an advertisement in the *Daily Mirror*, 24 June 1915)

What might a man be expected to do which would affect his home life if he enrolled?

In early 1917 she went to the new Government Rolling Mills factory in Southampton. Here she witnessed an accident; munitions work could be

dangerous, with risks of explosions and damage to health from exposure to chemicals such as TNT.

Almost all the machines had been made in a rush and were unpainted; most of the lathes lacked guards over the gear wheels and all had 'War Finish' painted on the outside. A mill-wright came along one day to look at a lathe that was giving trouble, and the operator, not noticing that the mill-wright had his right hand on the gear wheels, started the lathe. I heard a yell behind me, and, looking round, saw the poor chap's hand go right through the gear wheels. It seemed to go through very slowly – it was agonising to watch – and the result was three compound fractures and the loss of the little finger. (*Three Years or the Duration*)

A girl working in the Gun Factory, Woolwich Arsenal, in May 1918. Note that the work seems to be heavy, and she is wearing protective overalls.

Why was a new factory in some ways more dangerous than an old one?

Children

During the war, with many fathers away in the army and mothers out at work for the first time, children spent more time on their own. While some became very grown up and responsible, others were wild and undisciplined; in the cities, one of the main tasks of the women police was to try to keep youngsters on the streets out of trouble. Children, especially from working-class homes or rural areas, often went to work themselves (usually part-time) either to help keep the family business or farm running, or to contribute whatever they could to the household finances. At school the girls helped the war effort by sewing and knitting, and those who were in the Scouts and Guides, often the more middle-class children, were given all sorts of tasks, such as acting as messengers, sentries, or lending a hand with agricultural work in the summer holidays (see p. 40).

Schoolgirls holding vegetables that they grew on allotments at school.

CHANGES AT SCHOOL

At St Margaret's School, Bushey, Hertfordshire, a boarding school for girls, the pupils wrote about the changes in their daily life in the school magazine:

> **The War! . . . . Each morning the Form Mistresses read a synopsis of the news to their Forms before work begins; many extra papers are being taken in . . . and maps, pictures and lists of heroes decorate the Form Rooms. . . . A very special interest attaches to First-Aid, Hygiene, and general Girl Guide work, many recruits having lately been added to the Guides.** (December 1914)

What does this show about the attitudes of the school and its pupils to the war?

POOR SCHOOL ATTENDANCE

The attendance for this week promises to be worse than last week's attendance. Four children are absent in the lower group through illness, two of the older boys have asked for the whole week to assist at home, while there are still requests for the assistance of other children. On account of the enlisting for war service of many who were engaged in agricultural work, many farmers find it impossible to obtain labour, and are frequently glad of such assistance as even school boys can afford. It is useless to expect good attendance under such circumstances. (From Headmaster's Log Book, 1914, Chevithorne School, Tiverton, Devon)

Does your school have any old records which would show what the attendance was like in World War I? Although children were required by law to go to school regularly, generally till the age of fourteen, schools and local authorities knew that it was useless to insist on this during the war.

At St Margaret's, as everywhere else, the War has reduced the gardening staff, and we have to 'turn to' ourselves. . . . In response to the appeal that as much ground as possible should be used for planting vegetables, the ground near the Promenade and at the bottom of the New Field has been ploughed up, and each form given an 'allotment'. It is now a common sight to see people, arrayed in overalls and armed with huge forks and spades, trudging to the New Field, to dig. We are eagerly anticipating the time when we shall be able to have potatoes and vegetables out of our allotments for dinner! (1917-1918)

In the photograph you can see girls from another school proud y displaying the vegetables they have grown.

A BIRMINGHAM CHILDHOOD

Joseph Higtor was seven when the war began. His father enlisted immediately, and his mother found that she couldn't cope with running a shop in Coventry as well as looking after her six children. Three of the children went to live with an aunt nearby, and she took the other three, including Joseph, to live in Birmingham with her, near relatives. The family was very poor.

We couldn't afford fresh milk; we always had condensed milk. We used to look upon the houses in the terrace who had fresh milk as rich people really. Meals were very ordinary, no variety. The main diet was bread, with lard – as kids we used to put pepper and salt on

COPING WITH EMERGENCIES

In the war, older children often had to look after the little ones. A London tram conductress, delayed by an air raid, arrived home late:

She found that her eldest child, a little girl of seven-and-a-half, had got her four little brothers and sisters out of bed at the beginning of the air raid, had dressed them, brought them downstairs, gathered them all under the kitchen table, had lit a candle, and was reading to them out of the Bible. She had learnt at school what might be done in taking cover. (Henry Luke Paget, Bishop of Stepney, *Records of the Raids*, 1918)

it! I always did a part-time job. I can remember my first job was with a jewellers, and I had to go in the morning before school and clean the long brass curb in front of the window. Dinner-times I used to go there and do all their errands. Any money that I could bring into the house was very useful indeed. We kids didn't buy a lot, because we never had many halfpennies or pennies. But of course there was a tremendous amount of swapping – you would swap things five or six times. If you bought a couple of comics on Monday, by the end of the week you would probably have read about ten. (Memories recalled for this book in 1984)

From this section, and others in the book, make a list of jobs and tasks (paid or unpaid) which children would have been able to do to help their families and the war effort in general.

Soldiers in Britain

Not all soldiers were away fighting abroad. Many, including some from other parts of the British Empire, were posted in Britain for training. Some were "billeted" in family homes, while others lived in camps or in buildings such as hotels which had been turned into hostels. There were also injured soldiers to be nursed; in World War I approximately 750,000 men in the British troops were killed and over one and a half million wounded, many of whom came back to be looked after in hospitals in Britain.

BRINGING HOME WOUNDED SOLDIERS

Here is an early account of how soldiers were taken to hospital. Later, as the casualties grew heavier, they were brought into other British ports as well.

> All the hospital ships proceed to Southampton, where there is a special staff for the reception and distribution of the wounded. The arrangements are under the control of the Surgeon-General, who has at his command twelve ambulance trains. . . . Twice a week telegrams are received from all the larger military and Territorial Force general hospitals stating the number of beds vacant in each.
>
> As the military hospitals get filled up arrangements have been made for transferring sick and wounded from them to various hospitals arranged by voluntary effort. (*Daily Mirror*, 28 September 1914)

HOSPITALS

Extra hospitals were soon needed to cope with all the injured men. Anything from a stately home to

CANADIANS

Folkestone was a centre for many Canadian soldiers in training. Their stay influenced people in the town:

> You forgot to say 'Yes', because 'Sure!' was much more fashionable, and you never spoke of having a good meal. 'Good eats' was the correct equivalent. So, too, did our young people try to imitate the 'semi-nasal twang' they thought so 'fetching' and learnt to dance and 'rag' and sway as their

the local swimming baths could usefully be adapted.

> There are an amazing number of great houses, both in town and country, that have been stripped of their luxurious trappings and are now the soul of hygiene and whitewash, full of the halt and maimed in the blue and grey suits and red ties that have become so pathetically familiar to us. I know of one house in a great London thoroughfare that was once sparsely inhabited by a wealthy family of two. When the war called us all to sacrifice, the family of two dismissed the small army of servants, sold its valuable pictures and furniture, and offered the house to the War Office as a hospital.

Mrs Alphonse Courtlander included this in her account as a nurse in World War I, which appears in *Women War Workers* (1917). She describes the hospital uniform that soldiers wore. What was it? Can you find out if any buildings in your area were used as hospitals or convalescent homes at the time?

A group of soldiers from the Royal Engineers stationed in Buxton, lining up proudly on a bridge they have just finished building in the local park. This was done as a training project; they might need to put up a bridge quickly when fighting abroad.

Transatlantic friends would have them do. (Ernest J Mackay in *Folkestone during the War*, edited by J.C. Carlile)

A buffet run by volunteers for soldiers at Paddington Station, London. Troops would often arrive home on leave tired and hungry. The Motor Transport Volunteer Service was founded to help them travel across London:
"Since its inception, it has been the means of transporting across London over 225,000 men, during the hours when there are no other vehicles available. Before the MTV began their operations, soldiers arriving in London in the middle of the night . . . had to tramp through the streets, cold and hungry. . . . Now their case is very different. Free buffets remain open all night, and the lorries and cars of the MTV carry them quickly to their destination." (Illustrated London News, 7 July 1917)

BILLETING

When a regiment came to train in a district, householders were often invited to take soldiers into their homes. If there was not enough accommodation available, they might be forced to do so in any case. Many families were pleased to help and, in fact, people in Buxton, Derbyshire, were very annoyed when, after they had offered to be "billets", all the soldiers were put up at a large hotel instead. In Berkshire, Peggy Hamilton's parents took in soldiers. Here are the official instructions they received. (You can read more about Peggy on p. 32)

Instructions to Occupiers of Houses upon whom Troops are Billeted

1. You are required to provide cover for the number of men allocated to you for billets by the Police.
2. If the Police inform you that you are to provide food for the soldiers billeted on you the meals must be provided per scale which is exhibited in the Police Station.
3. In the above case, the sum of two shillings and sixpence per day will be paid to you for each man billeted on you. If you are not required to provide food, the sum of ninepence per day will be paid to you for each soldier billeted on you. The accommodation required to be provided for the latter sum is as follows:

Lodgings and attendance, and candles, vinegar, salt: the use of the fire, and the necessary utensils for the dressing and eating of meat.

What sort of service did householders have to provide for the soldiers? Why do you think it had to be set down in detail?

Keeping in Touch

Soldiers serving abroad kept in touch with their families by writing letters. Lancelot Spicer, an officer in the Yorkshire Light Infantry, wrote home to his parents noting some of the difficulties and the pleasures of communicating by post. What are they?

September 12th 1915: It is really very hard to know what to say, since as soon as one thinks of anything interesting to say . . . one suddenly remembers one must not say it because the Censor might not approve . . .

Oct 15th 1915: 'We get letters here very regularly – we can almost rely on having them every day and certainly every other day, which is remarkably good considering the way we move about. I must say I have never appreciated letters more in all my life than I do out here, and I know everybody says the same. (From *Letters from France 1915-1918*)

This cigarette advertisement contains a made-up letter from a young woman to her husband or brother. It reflects the kinds of things that families would want to write to their relatives in the army – what are they?

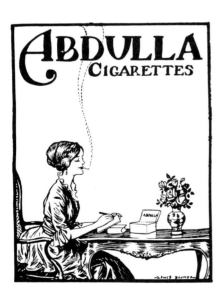

The public was encouraged to help supply items for soldiers at the front.

We knitted socks (some of them of unusual shape), waistcoats, helmets, comforters, mitts, body belts. We knitted at theatres, in trains and trams, in pubs and parlours, in the intervals of eating in restaurants or serving in canteens. Men knitted, children knitted. . . . It was soothing to our nerves to knit, and comforting to think that the result of our labours might save some men something of hardship and misery, for always the knowledge of what our men suffered haunted us. (Mrs C.S. Peel, *How We Lived Then*, 1929)

Readers of *The Daily Mirror* have now contributed 18,000 blankets for the comfort of our soldiers.

This is a splendid achievement, but we want still more – very many more – for our fighting heroes.

These men have sacrificed much – in many cases all – for their country.

Surely you who stay at home recognise your duty to do all you can to help them in their struggles?

Many of our brave men are shivering through cold damp and sleepless nights – a hardship you can assist in avoiding by sending blankets.

We want Daily Mirror readers to raise the total of their contributions to 100,000 very soon. (*Daily Mirror*, 28 September 1914)

Suggestions for what should go in a parcel for a ➤ *soldier. Try to work out why each of these products would be appreciated.*

W & D Downey – Court Photographers, 61 Ebury St. London S.W. Begs to give notice to officers of His Majesty's Navy, Army and Auxiliary Forces that their studios will be available for the purpose of photographing them without sitting fees, from 9 to 6 daily until further notice. (Advertisement in *The Times*, 7 August 1914)

Why would men in the forces want to be photographed?

Separation and Bereavement

PARTING

When the war broke out, soldiers left by train in high spirits, singing patriotic songs and often drunk. But as the war progressed, and as many as 21,000 men were reported killed in a single day, leaving home became a gruelling experience. On her way home from work at the Woolwich Arsenal, Peggy Hamilton would see the following scene:

> Waterloo was a harrowing station to pass through. The platforms would be lined with troops on their way to the front. Pathetic little groups of relations would be clustered round them, bedraggled weeping women with babies in their arms . . . the men would be silent and stony-faced, standing beside their packs and rifles, as children cried and over everything lay a feeling of hopeless despair. (*Three Years or the Duration*, 1978)

A SONG ABOUT SAYING GOODBYE

Till We Meet Again

There's a song in the land of the lily
Each sweetheart has heard with a sigh
Over high garden walls
This sweet echo falls
As a loving boy whispers 'good-bye'.

CHORUS
Smile the while you kiss me sad adieu
When the clouds roll away I'll come to
  you;
Then the skies will seem more blue,
Down in lover's lane, my dearie.
Wedding bells will ring so merrily,
Every tear will be a memory,

A SOLDIER'S LEAVE

Soldiers could usually come home on leave every few months, and then had to part with their families all over again. Robert Saunders, a schoolmaster in Sussex, described his son Ron's leave. Why was it such a painful experience?

> We did not ask Ron to have [a photo] taken when he was home, it is much nicer to picture him as he was in his last photo before he had gone through the terrible experiences all our men at the front have to bear. Whatever newspaper writers may say you may take my word for it no one can ever look the same again after seeing the awful slaughter of a modern battle field . . . and living in the trenches. I sat and watched Ron when he came home and tried to note the change in him. . . . He used to sit hunched up towards the fire, every now and then holding his hands to the blaze, his face seemed unnaturally long, nose prominent, black marks under his eyes, hair rough and badly cut, and quite content just to

> So wait and pray each night for me,
> Till we meet again.
>
> Tho' goodbye means the birth of a
>   tear-drop
> Hello! means the birth of a smile,
> And the smile will erase
> The tear blighting trace
> When we meet in the after-awhile.
> (Words by Raymond B. Egan)

What would the appeal of this song have been?

sit and talk. . . . He doesn't want to go in the trenches again, and would gladly return to civil life again. We did all we could to strengthen him up but the time was all too short, and though he tried not to show it, he felt parting keenly. (From a letter to his elder son in Canada, 12 December 1915)

Can you find out what the "trenches" were?

THOSE WHO NEVER RETURNED

List of men who had died were published in the newspapers every day, and close relatives were usually informed by telegram. Later the soldier's possessions would be sent home. Vera Brittain, was engaged to Roland Leighton and she, and his sister Clare, recalled the terrible task of dealing with his possessions after he was killed.

As I write this I find myself back in childhood. It is a cold morning in January and I am in the garden of our cottage in Sussex. My father is with me. I carry two heavy kettles. They are filled with boiling water, for we are about to bury the tunic – blood-stained and bullet-riddled – in which Roland has been killed. Father watches the windows of the house, for my mother must not see this tunic. . . . I am to thaw the frozen earth so that it may be buried out of sight. (Clare Leighton: preface to *Chronicle of Youth*)

I had no idea before of the aftermath of an officer's death, or what the returned kit . . . really meant. It was terrible. . . .

A mother prepares to say goodbye to her son as he returns to the "front" after leave at home.

The only things untouched by damp or mud or mould were my photographs, kept carefully in an envelope, and his leather cigarette case, with a few cigarettes and tiny photo of his Mother. . . . The very worst things we found were one or two quite small unpaid bills. (Vera Brittain, *Chronicle of Youth*)

Some public buildings, such as town halls or railway stations, have a memorial plaque listing the men who lived or worked there who were killed in the Great War. See if you can find one in your district.

If you look through other sections of this book you will find other ways in which separation affected daily and family life. Can you trace any of your family history at the time to discover if any of your relatives were in the army, and, if so, whether they returned home alive or were killed in action?

Public Health and Morale

The chances of winning a war are greater if the public morale is high – that is to say, if people feel cheerful, fit and optimistic. Morale was certainly high at the beginning of the war, but it became increasingly difficult for the general population to keep their confidence in the war effort. The war went on far longer than expected, and many people had to cope with the grief of learning that a close friend or relative had died in the fighting. Extra work taken on to help the war effort caused strain and exhaustion, and late in the war an outbreak of influenza undermined the health of many; between 1918 and 1919 (just after the war) over 150,000 people died from the illness.

Shut Out Infection!

TOXOL

The highest grade British Lysol. Unquestionably the best germicide, antiseptic, and disinfectant for general use. It overcomes offensive odours, purifies the atmosphere, counteracts infection, and destroys all disease germs and bacilli. Toxol is unsurpassed for the sick room and general household use. Safe and economical.

8d., 10½d., 1/6 & 2/9 per bottle.

TOXOL SOAP minimises the danger of infection and contagion. It contains five per cent. of Boots The Chemists TOXOL, the celebrated germicide, antiseptic, and disinfectant.

Toxol Soap is perfectly saponified, and contains no free alkali. It is a pure soap, free from injurious chemicals.

Toxol Soap is just as ideal for washing tender surfaces and keeping cuts and abrasions surgically clean as it is for toilet, bath, and nursery use. It is both healthful and cleansing.

Toxol Soap is most economical. Both in the sick room and home it acts as a barrier against infection. Begin to-day to use this splendid safeguard.

Toxol Toilet Soap

4½d. per tablet. 1/1½ per box of three tablets.

Made and sold only by Boots The Chemists ::: 555 Branches throughout the country.

Boots Pure Drug Co. Limited.

TONICS

Manufacturers used the fact that people were extra-tired and anxious to help them sell their medicines and tonics:

> **FATIGUE**
> Those who have responded to their country's call for men of good will to serve in ways to which they are not

This advertisement is playing on a common fear of the time to encourage people to buy antiseptic soap. What is it?

INFLUENZA

'Flu was a more serious illness in the early twentieth century than it is today. Robert Saunders wrote about how it was affecting his school and village in Sussex in October 1918. Why do you think many families would have found an outbreak of 'flu particularly hard to cope with during the war?

> When I opened school on Monday I had 92 absent, so after wiring the Medical Officer, we had to close for a fortnight. Influenza is rampant in Sussex, nearly all the schools around are closed, and there is hardly a house that isn't affected. . . . There have been several distressing deaths in the district, of mothers who while nursing other members of the family, suddenly died of heart failure caused by Influenza. Everybody is trying some remedy or other, the Chemists are flourishing, but after all the only proven safeguard is bed and nourishing food.

> accustomed know the strain of unusual fatigue.
> The special constable who has perhaps never stood for hours at a time in the night in one spot or patrolled a small beat, is tiring an entirely new set of muscles, while the strain of vigilant attention tells severely on his nerves. Much relief, and renewed vigour for the performance of the day's ordinary work, will be gained by a little extra feeding. Take regularly. . . . 'Byrogen'.
> (Advertisement in *Illustrated London News,* 18 August 1917)

WAR-WEARINESS

Soldiers in the war had to face many hardships and dangers, and they wanted to feel that the people in Britain were supporting them in their struggle. Lancelot Spicer had been in the army for two and a half years when he wrote this letter home to his parents in February 1918:

> Now I come to what I call the serious part of your letter and that is that you say that many people at home are very depressed about the war. Now that is a very serious thing – it means that 'morale' at home is bad. One of the first and most essential things about the Army is that in order to fight well it must have good morale . . . if your morale is bad, you won't be able to bear [the strain] and you'll give way and want to make peace. . . . The one thing that is absolutely necessary is that every one including all those at home should do everything they possibly can to help in the defeat of Germany. . . . And it isn't only the lower classes who apparently are not doing all they might, it's people of the educated and wealthier classes, who ought to know much better. (*Letters from France 1915-1918*)

What does this tell you about his attitudes to people of different social backgrounds, and why do you think he expects certain classes "to know much better"?

Fashions and Clothing

In Edwardian times, leading up to the war, fashions in clothes had been elaborate. Women wore dresses with long, full skirts and petticoats, and their hair was usually grown long and swept up into an imposing style. During the war, with shortages of material and with many women doing manual work, it became practical to make dresses with a straighter line and which were worn somewhat shorter. Some women cut their hair short, and by the 1920s the fashion for short hair and skirts was firmly established. Some women even wore trousers, which was almost unheard of previously. Men in the armed forces who were in Britain for training or on leave were at first proud to be seen in spick and span uniform, but later they liked to look more bedraggled as this would show they had been on active service and win them admiration. Social manners changed during the war; it became more acceptable for young girls to go out alone without an older friend or relative to "chaperone" them, and for women to drive, drink in pubs, and eat out without a male escort. This is because women were leading more active and less sheltered lives.

EXHIBITION
of WAR ECONOMY DRESS.
MUST · BE · SEEN · BY · EVERYONE
Grafton Galleries, Bond Street.
10 to 6. From 3rd to 31st August (Inclusive)

1818   1918

The National Standard Dress will be demonstrated by Mrs Allan Hawkey, The Inventor, who will Lecture Daily.

MANY OTHER ATTRACTIONS
Orchestra will play daily.
Admission 1/3d Inclusive of Tax.

_____ LONDON FASHIONS _____

Many changes have come over London with the progress of the war. . . . Thus, for example, the afternoon drive in the Park, which used to be an affair of gay dresses and fluttering parasols, mingled with shiny top-hats and immaculate tailoring, has now developed into a very different scene. . . . The fripperies of fashion have given place to much simpler feminine costumes. . . . Woman is now no longer an ornamental passenger. The goddess has moved to the wheel. Instead of being driven, she drives; and her favoured guests are men who have fought and suffered in order to keep her and the country safe. (Illustrated London News 1 September 1917)

What changes has the writer noted?

What is the purpose of this "economy dress"? Can you find some examples of dresses worn in 1900-14 and compare them with this one?

WOMEN IN UNIFORM

Uniforms were commonly worn in the war by women for the first time. What do you think of the ones described here? See if you can find other pictures, in this book and elsewhere, of women in uniforms and working clothes during the war. Peggy Hamilton recalls the uniforms of female workers in the Southampton munitions factory (see page 24-25):

We in the toolroom were given thick, voluminous cotton overalls with caps to match. The overalls were hot and bulky and tied round the waist with anything we could find. We looked like bundles of old rags. We had to have our hair covered to prevent it catching in the machinery, but these caps were also heavy and hot and particularly uncomfortable in the summer. . . . The greasers had the worst outfit of all. It consisted of enormous, baggy bloomers. . . . Only the crane girls had a smart outfit. They looked quite smashing in their khaki coats, caps and breeches, especially one who wore lacy openwork stockings and high-heeled shoes with her uniform. (*Three Years or the Duration – The Memoirs of a Munition Worker 1914-18,* published 1978)

Why do you think there were different uniforms for the different jobs?

WORKING-CLASS GIRLS

The war did much to reduce the difference between the upper and lower classes. Working-class girls, with better pay, were able to buy more clothes and improve their appearance.

Some items, like sugar boxes, were made only during the war. Because sugar was in such short supply, it was considered polite to take your sugar with you if you went out to tea.

An observant person visiting at one of the great London hospitals, on a Sunday in November 1918, standing alongside to let the crowd of friends and relations pass before him up the flight of steps leading to the entrance door, failed to see one shabby pair of shoes and any but the neatest stockings, many of them silk. Before the war, if girls had gone to the factory dressed as they dress to-day they would have been pelted with filth, denounced as shameless hussies or worse. (Mrs C.S. Peel, *How We Lived Then,* 1929)

(The stockings they had worn previously were of heavy wool.)

Food

Food could not be brought into the country easily, since many ships were in use for military purposes and those that were left were in danger of being attacked at sea. Some people tried to hoard supplies of food, and this added to the problem, so that food shortages, especially of potatoes, sugar and meat, became common. Prices rose very fast; a loaf of bread went up from 5½d to 8d during the first few days of the war. Eventually, in 1918, the Government introduced rationing to try to make sure that food supplies were shared out fairly at a reasonable price.

SHORTAGES AND RESTRICTIONS

21st March 1916
Sugar is increasingly difficult to buy, and many grocers won't sell it unless you buy tea at the same time. . . . I have quite given up sugar in tea, but I can't say I enjoy a cup of tea as I used to.

15th February 1917
Things are being done gradually in England to overcome the Drink Evil. The Public Houses are open only during certain hours . . . the quantity of whisky etc allowed to be distilled has been several times reduced, and the percentage of alcohol lowered while the price has been raised. A 4/– bottle of whisky costs 5/6d, a bottle of beer formerly 4½d is 6½d, so that except for the rich, Temperance [moderation] has to be followed.

9th April 1917
[In London] I saw the first potato

WAR-TIME RECIPES

The Government tried to give helpful advice to housewives on making the most of their food. See what you think of these suggested ingredients for "War-Time Soup":

All outer leaves and peelings and tops and tails of vegetables, all fruit peelings, stones and cores, all saucepan and dish rinsings, bread crusts, remains of suet, batter and milky puddings (but not jam or sweet puddings), cheese and bacon rinds, skim milk, sour milk, remains of sauces (not sweet sauces) or gravy, vegetable water, margarine (if liked), pepper, salt, water. Every economical housewife should have War-Time Soup constantly going; it is both delicious and nourishing and, above all, cheap.
(Ministry of Food recipe quoted in Mrs C.S. Peel, *How We Lived Then*, 1929)

queue. . . . Most of the green grocers have a big notice up 'No Potatoes this week', but I find many of them have a small supply out of sight which they supply in 2lbs lots to their regular customers. (Extracts from letters from Robert Saunders to his son)

How are the Government, the public and the shopkeepers trying to deal with the problems he mentions? Controls over drink were made because the Government thought that too much drinking was causing laziness and accidents in factories.

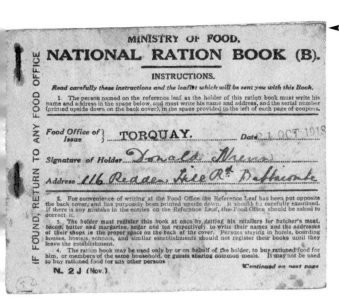

A ration card. This contained stamps which had to be handed in to the shopkeeper when buying meat, butter, sugar, tea and jam.

We risk our lives to bring you food. It's up to you not to waste it.

"A Message from our Seamen"

A Government food poster to encourage people to use their food supplies sensibly. Boats carrying food were in danger of being attacked and sunk by the enemy.

JAM FOR TEA

Much of the fruit grown in Britain was made into jam which was sent to soldiers abroad (see page 20). Other ways of making jam for the people at home had to be found, and it was generally the poorer families, such as Joseph Higton's in Birmingham, that had to put up with the substitutes.

> Tea was usually bread and jam. The jam that was sold in those days was mainly plum and blackberry and apple. There were other jams but they were regarded by us as luxuries. There was apricot, and blackcurrant jam – I used to think I was in heaven if I had those! But we only had them occasionally. Many of the jams at that time were made with marrow – marrow and ginger, and marrow with this and that and, oh dear, they were not nice at all!
> (Memories recalled for this book, 1984)

Popular Entertainment

Entertainment did a great deal to inform people about the war and to keep their spirits up. There were around 3,000 cinemas in 1914, and as well as popular silent comedy and cowboy films they also had news films and stories containing propaganda (see page 15). Songs were much enjoyed in music halls, concerts or round the piano at home. Many had a patriotic flavour, as you can see from the examples here. People also liked to go to meetings (such as economy cooking demonstrations) and Bridge Clubs, since with black-outs and fuel shortages it could be cold and gloomy at home.

A CHARITY CONCERT

A patriotic concert was given on Saturday afternoon, on the Slopes, by the Burbage Pond, when a choice selection of music was performed. The local Boy Scouts were present in good numbers [and] rendered excellent services by selling programmes and collecting. The proceeds were in aid of the Local Relief Fund, and about £10 was realised. (*Buxton Advertiser*, 5 September 1914)

The Fund was probably to help families who were facing hardship because of the war.

FICTION

This is the introduction to a serial story in a magazine, *The Vivid* (February 1916). What does it tell you about popular attitudes in war-time?

**The One Who Stayed Behind –
A Dramatic Tale of Love and War
By Henry St John Cooper – The First
Chapters in Brief**
Dan Eddrington, son of John Eddrington . . . stays behind, and endures the taunts of everyone because he has not joined the Army. His brother, Steve, enlists. Dan is needed at home, because his father has mental lapses, although the old man is unaware of it. Only the two brothers . . . share the secret.

Joan, John Eddrington's ward, was formerly engaged to Dan, but, unable to account for his apparent cowardice, returns his ring.

Dan is able to help his King and Country. He discovers a secret petrol store for enemy submarines. . . .
Through careful watching, he finds out who the spies are . . .

SONGS

Here are verses from four popular songs. You will see that they all have a war theme.

Boys in Khaki, Boys in Blue
Boys in Khaki, boys in blue,
Here's the best of jolly good luck to you!
You're all right in love or war;
You'll get there again just the same as
    you've done before.
Boys in Khaki, boys in blue,
It's no idle boast or brag,
When we get you both together, there's
    going to be dirty weather
For anyone who tramples on the flag!

This song commemorates a famous event in the war. ▶
Can you find out what it was?

Your King and Your Country Need You
Come on Tommy – come on Jack,
We'll guard the Home till you come
    back,
Come on Sandy, come on Pat,
For you're true blue!
Down your tools and leave your
    benches,
Say goodbye to all the wenches,
Take your gun and 'May God speed
    you!'
For your King and your Country need
    you!

Farewell Isabelle
Farewell Isabelle! Isabelle,
Don't let it grieve you,
I've got to go!
Farewell Isabelle! Isabelle,
I've got to leave you
To face the foe.
You know very well, Isabelle
As the battle I go through,
I shall do my best when I'm in it
As I won you!

Ev'ry Day is One Day Nearer
Ev'ry day is one day nearer
To the day when there's no more war.
Fighting done, vict'ry won,
And the world at peace once more.
Ev'ry day the skies are clearer,
And the storm clouds sail away,
There's a good time coming, a good time
    coming,
Coming nearer ev'ry day.

KITCHENER
AND THE
SEVEN HUNDRED

THE LOSS OF

H.M.S. Hampshire
JUNE 5th, 1916

Words by
Rev. J. MOUNTAIN, D.D.

Music by
Capt. COLIN M. CAMPBELL, R.E.(T.)

Revised by ROBERT HARKNESS

COPYRIGHT   PRICE THREEPENCE NET

LONDON : MORGAN & SCOTT Ltd.
12, Paternoster Buildings, E.C.

WORDS ONLY, on folded Art card, with portrait of Lord Kitchener, One Penny each.

What does this advertisement tell you both about the kind of entertainment people usually liked, and what could be offered in its place?

The PET of the FLEET

JACK'S THEATRE & MUSIC-HALL
are keeping him bright and cheerful in the grim North Sea. Are YOU having your usual enjoyment now that war has brought in its trail scarcity (and mediocrity) of concerts and theatres and variety shows? By means of 'His Master's Voice' British-made Gramophone you can have at home the world's greatest artists from Caruso to Lauder: or a stirring patriotic concert with Radford singing "Fall in!" the Cecilian Quartette singing "Tipperary," the Coldstreamers playing the Allies' War Songs, and so on *ad lib.*—no booking, "dressing," or taxi-bill! All dealers will give you a Free Concert.

TABLE GRAND, No. 9 in Mahogany—internal horn, grand reproduction £16 16s.

Write us for Illustrated Brochures of Records and Instruments
The Gramophone Co. Ltd
HAYES · MIDDLESEX

"His Master's Voice"
GRAMOPHONE—*the theatre at home!*

The Armistice

On 11 November 1918, fighting between Germany and Britain came to an end. People were very relieved; the war had been exhausting, with long working hours, food and fuel shortages, and worry about male relatives and friends serving abroad. Not all problems ceased on this date; food rationing carried on for about another year, and women often had to give up their well-paid employment when men returned home. But Armistice Day was celebrated with great enthusiasm.

Armistice celebrations in a city street.

CELEBRATIONS AT ST MARGARET'S SCHOOL, BUSHEY

On Monday, November 11th, when the Armistice was signed, St Margaret's went quite mad with joy.

The news reached us about mid-day, and we all went into Chapel for a short Thanksgiving Service. After this all the Guides marched past the Union Jack, saluting.

We made as much noise as possible, and after we had blown all the fire-whistles, rung the gong, and all the bells, we went out to the terrace, where the Orchestra joined us, and to its accompaniment we sang all the National Songs we could think of. Then we made a triumphal procession all over the ground and across to Hill Brow, the Orchestra in front, playing lustily, and the School following, singing. (From St Margaret's school magazine)

CELEBRATIONS IN SUSSEX

In a Sussex village, Robert Saunders also enjoyed the day:

The news reached Fletching about 11.40am, and was soon brought down to school where the Union Jack was at once hoisted and the children cheered loud enough to be heard all over the parish. When I came home to dinner everyone was out putting up flags and colours, and though people were excited, there was no noise till a scratch team started to ring the bells. . . . After tea our church clock, which had been silent all through the War, struck at 6, and has continued striking day and night. . . . To all here it meant so much, and sounded like the voice of an old friend returning from the grave. (From a letter to his son William in Canada, 16 November 1918)

Why do you think the clock had been silent? Can you find examples elsewhere in the book of restrictions that would have been lifted at the end of the war?

RETURNING SOLDIERS

Here is a poem by P.H.B. Lyon, celebrating his return from fighting with the Durham Light Infantry. What special pleasures does he find in coming home? You will also find an indication of the hopes that many people had at the end of the war – what were they?

Now to be Still and Rest

Now to be still and rest, while the heart
    remembers,
All that it learned and loved in the days
    long past,
To stoop and warm our hands at the
    fallen embers,
Glad to have come the long way's end at
    last.

Now to awake, and feel no regret at
    waking,
Knowing the shadowy days are white
    again,
To draw our curtains and watch the
    slow dawn breaking
Silver and grey on English field and
    lane.

Now to fulfil our dreams in woods
    and meadows
Treading the well-loved paths – to
    pause and cry

'So, even so I remember it' – seeing the
    shadows
Weave on the distant hills their
    tapestry.

Now to rejoice in children and join their
    laughter,
Turning our hearts once more to the
    fairy strain,
To hear our names on voices we love,
    and after
Turn with a smile to sleep and our
    dreams again.

Then – with a new-born strength, the
    sweet rest over,
Gladly to follow the great white road
    once more,
To work with a song on our lips and the
    heart of a lover,
Building a city of peace on the wastes of
    war.

(From *Turn Fortune*, Constable Publishers)
1914-1918)

43

Map

SCOTLAND

NORTH SEA

•Glasgow

NORTHERN
IRELAND

•Hebburn on Tyne

Scarborough

IRISH SEA

•Manchester   Cleethorpes
           •Buxton
Macclesfield•
           •Leek

E N G L A N D
Birmingham   Mattishall•
•   •Coventry   Bury St
                              Edmunds   Lowestoft•
            •Leamington   •Stowmarket
W A L E S   Cambridge• Sudbury•
                        Braintree•
                  Bushey•
            Harrow• •Willesden Woolwich•
            Shoreditch•   •Sheerness
                  •Frimley   Blean•
            Haslemere•   Folkestone•
•Tiverton   Southampton• Fletching•
                  Portsmouth

E N G L I S H   C H A N N E L

Date List

1914

4 August — War declared between Britain and Germany.

10 August — Special Constabulary formed to help war emergency on home front.

September — Battle of the Marne in France; a success for the Allies.

1915

January — Trench warfare sets in, with each side digging themselves in along a 400-mile line on the French frontier.

March — Industrial strikes by the Clydeside engineers and Mersey dockers. Start of the campaign against drinking. Women willing to work invited to register their names.

April — Germans use poison gas at Ypres for the first time. Allies launch attack in the Dardanelles (Turkish coast).

May — First Zeppelin raid on London. Sinking of the passenger ship the *Lusitania* by the Germans. Ministry of Munitions formed.

1916

February — First woman "clippie" (bus or tram conductress) goes to work.

May — Conscription Act. Summer Time, or "Daylight Saving Time" introduced for first time.

1 July — British launch attack on Germans on the river Somme.

December — "Government bread" introduced; all bread to be made to Government specifications.

1917

February — Germans declare all-out sea warfare.

March — Revolution in Russia.

6 April — America joins war on side of the Allies.

7 April — Meat rationing starts.

25 May — First German aeroplane raid on Britain.

13 June — Worst daylight bombing raid on London.

November — First British mass tank attack in Cambrai, Belgium.

December — Peace negotiations began between Russia and Germany.

1918

16 February — Women over 30 given the vote.

25 February — Rationing of basic food and price controls introduced.

21 March — Germans launch new offensive on Western Front under command of Hindenburg.

8 August — Allies success in battle on the river Somme.

27-30 September — Allies break the "Hindenburg Line" resistance.

October — German fleet mutinies and the Kaiser abdicates.

11 November — Germany accepts the Allies' terms for ending the war; an armistice is declared.

Difficult Words

aliens	foreigners.
armistice	a truce, an agreement to stop fighting.
arsenal	a building for storing weapons and ammunition.
bed-mackintosh	rubber sheet.
bereavement	loss of someone close to you.
billet	lodgings for soldiers.
breeches	trousers worn to just below the knee.
censorship	cutting out all or part of material in letters, newspapers etc, in case it betrays secrets to the enemy or could damage the war effort in some way.
conscription	making it compulsory for people to join military services if they are asked to do so.
conviction	belief.
Dardenelles	the narrow channel of water that separates European from Asian Turkey; scene of an important campaign in 1915.
dressing	bandage or covering for a wound.
embers	glowing coals or ashes.
fripperies	showy and ornamental items of dress.
goose-step	the German marching step.
halt and maimed	injured.
hydroplane	a plane which could land on water.
hygiene	understanding how to keep healthy, especially through cleanliness.
immaculate	perfectly neat and clean.
impromptu	unplanned, on the spur of the moment.
impunity	without fear of punishment.
influenza	flu.
internee	someone detained during a war; usually applied to civilians from enemy countries.
lathe	a machine for rounding off metal or wood.
in league with	working with.
loch	lake.
mill-wright	in this case, a specialist engineer.
neutrality	used here to refer to a country which is not taking sides in a war.
pandemonium	a noisy and confused scene.
parasol	a lightweight umbrella used to keep off the sun.
pathetic	sad.
patriotism	supporting one's country.
pillage	seizing goods.
pneumonia	a serious illness affecting the chest and lungs.
requisitioning	use of power by Government to take possessions from private people – here to take what was needed for the war.
scarcity	shortage.
shrapnel	metal scattered from a bomb.
sweets of liberty	pleasures of freedom.
synopsis	a summary or short account.
taunts	scornful teasing.
temperance	used to mean not drinking alcohol.
thoroughfare	a road.
Tommy	nickname for British soldiers in World War I.
utensils	cutlery.

Money

There were 12 old pence (d) in a shilling (s) and 20 shillings in a pound (£). A shilling is equal to 5p.

Prices seem very low, but remember that wages were too. Don't compare prices with those of today, without looking at earnings then and now.

Book List

Books for Younger Readers

Hamilton, Peggy, *Three Years or the Duration – The Memoirs of a Munition Worker 1914-1918,* Peter Owen, 1978

Hoare, Robert, *World War One,* Macdonald, 1973 and 1983

Peel, Mrs. C. S., *How We Lived Then,* Lane, 1933

Tames, Richard, *The Great War,* B.T. Batsford Ltd, 1984

Warner, Philip, *Growing up in the First World War,* Wayland, 1980

Books for Older Readers

Brittain, Vera, *Chronicle of Youth,* Victor Gollancz, 1981

Brittain, Vera, *Testament of Youth,* Virago 1978

McMillan, James, *The Way it Was 1914-1934,* William Kimber

Marwick, Arthur, *Women at War 1914-1918,* Croom Helm 1977

Spicer, Lancelot Dykes, *Letters from France 1915-1918,* Robert York, 1979

Stevenson, John, *British Society 1914-1945,* Pelican Social History

Reference

The Times Atlas of World History, Times Books, 1978

Booklists

The Imperial War Museum, Lambeth Road, supplies booklists on different World War I topics. Some of the books and pamphlets listed are rare items which would only be available in the Museum Reading Room, but others could be ordered from your local library or traced in a reference library. Topics of particular interest are:

Airships (Booklist No. 1204)

British Women in the First World War (No. 1354)

Censorship during the First World War (No. 1144)

Conscientious Objectors in Britain 1914-1918 (No. 1025)

Espionage (No. 1321A)

The First World War (booklist for a student project – No. 1104)

First World War Literature (No. 1642)

First World War Poetry (No. 1295A)

Food Supplies and Rationing 1914-1918 – (No. 1151)

London 1914-18 (No. 1268)

Munition Production in Britain 1914-1918 (No. 1488)

Recruiting (No. 1252A)

Social History of Great Britain 1914-1918 (No. 1078A)

Index